COWBOY CAMPFIRE SONGS

ARRANGED BY LISLE CROWLEY

CONTENTS

Catalog #07-4083
ISBN# 1-56922-146-4

Printed in the United States of America
Produced by John L. Haag

Exclusive Selling Agent:

HAL•LEONARD®
CORPORATION
7777 W. BLUEMOUND RD. P.O. BOX 13819 MILWAUKEE, WI 53213

QUICK REFERENCE CHART

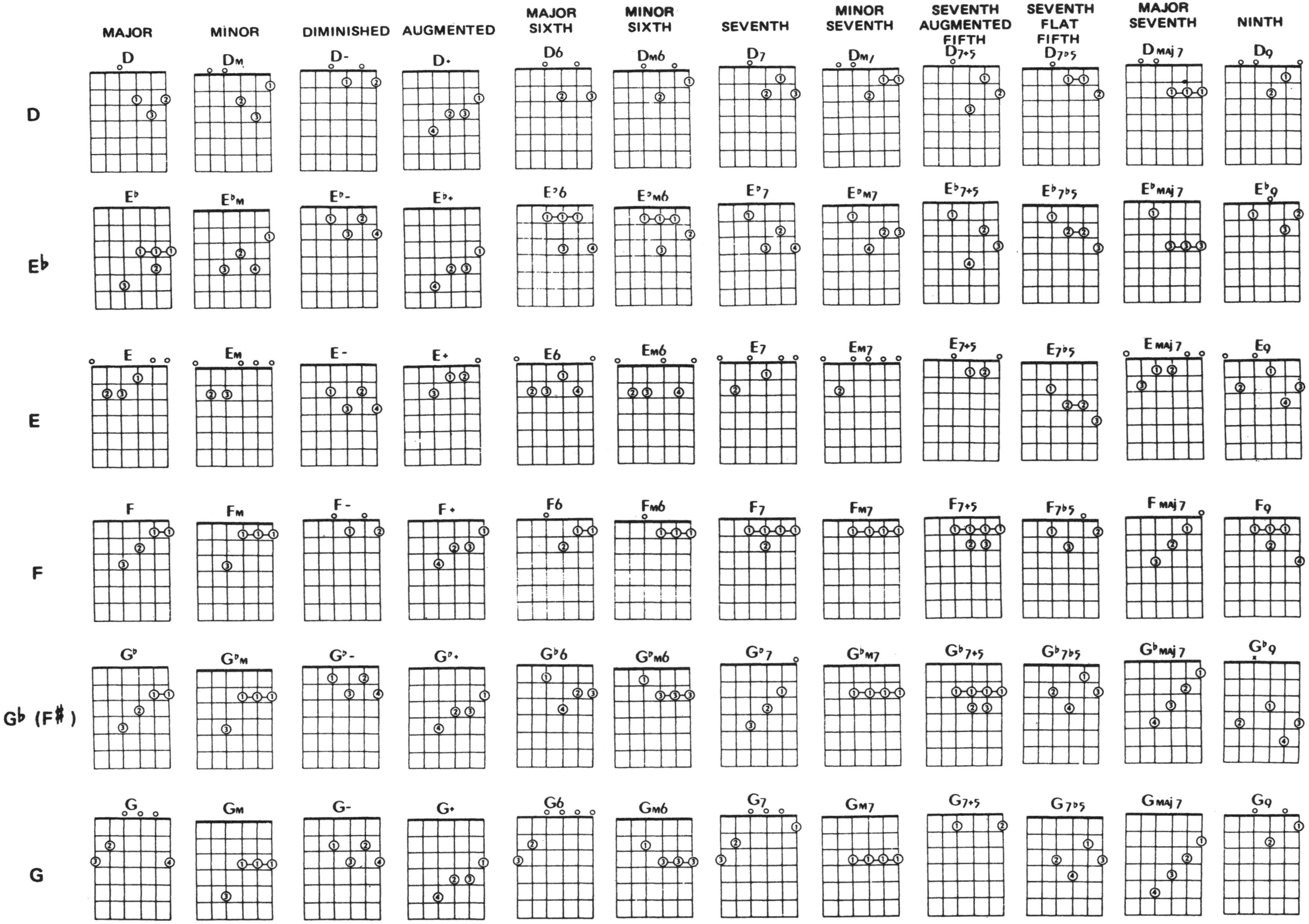
MAJOR
MINOR
DIMINISHED
AUGMENTED
MAJOR SIXTH
MINOR SIXTH
SEVENTH
MINOR SEVENTH
SEVENTH AUGMENTED FIFTH
SEVENTH FLAT FIFTH
MAJOR SEVENTH
NINTH
D
D
Dm
D-
D+
D6
Dm6
D7
Dm7
D7+5
D7♭5
Dmaj7
D9
E♭
E♭
E♭m
E♭-
E♭+
E♭6
E♭m6
E♭7
E♭m7
E♭7+5
E♭7♭5
E♭maj7
E♭9
E
E
Em
E-
E+
E6
Em6
E7
Em7
E7+5
E7♭5
Emaj7
E9
F
F
Fm
F-
F+
F6
Fm6
F7
Fm7
F7+5
F7♭5
Fmaj7
F9
G♭ (F♯)
G♭
G♭m
G♭-
G♭+
G♭6
G♭m6
G♭7
G♭m7
G♭7+5
G♭7♭5
G♭maj7
G♭9
G
G
Gm
G-
G+
G6
Gm6
G7
Gm7
G7+5
G7♭5
Gmaj7
G9

LISLE CROWLEY has been a professional musician for the last ten years since graduating from Utah State University where he recieved his B.M. in guitar performance. He has performed many different styles of music with different groups, but has focused on fingerstyle guitar. His credits include commercials, educational films and an aerobic video he composed and performed the music for. He has owned his own teaching studio and is currently teaching guitar for Dixie College and Tuacahn Center for the Arts. He is presently working on the release of his first C.D.

ABILENE

TRADITIONAL

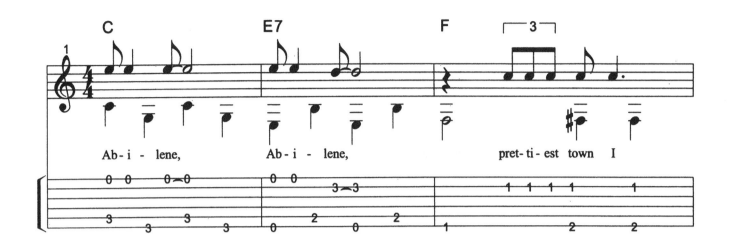

Ab - i - lene, Ab - i - lene, pret - ti - est town I

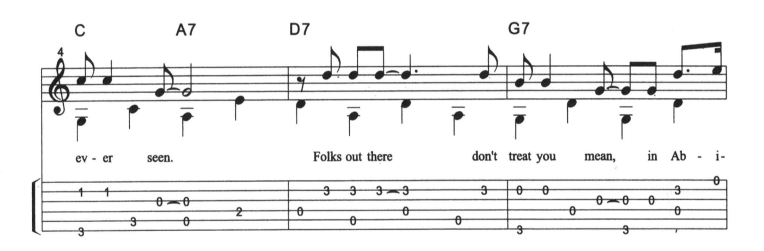

ev - er seen. Folks out there don't treat you mean, in Ab - i -

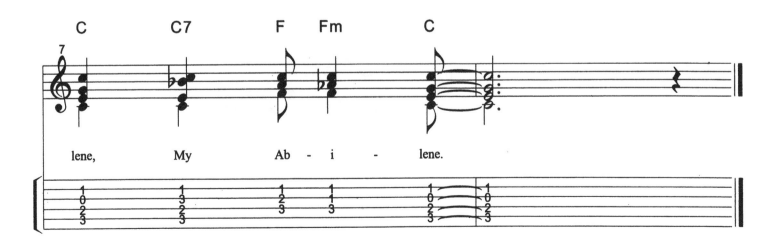

lene, My Ab - i - lene.

BURY ME NOT ON THE LONE PRAIRIE

WORDS AND MUSIC BY E. H. CHAPIN

A

"Oh, bur - y me not   on the lone prai -

E

rie,"   These words came low

A

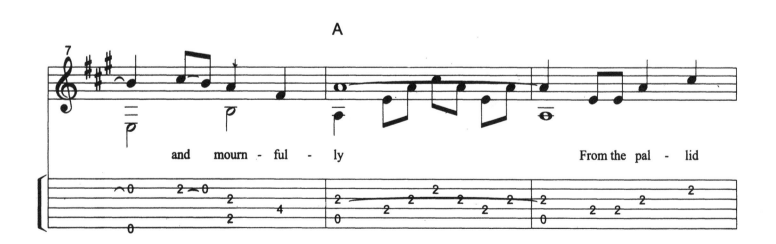

and mourn - ful - ly   From the pal - lid

lips   of a youth who lay

E7

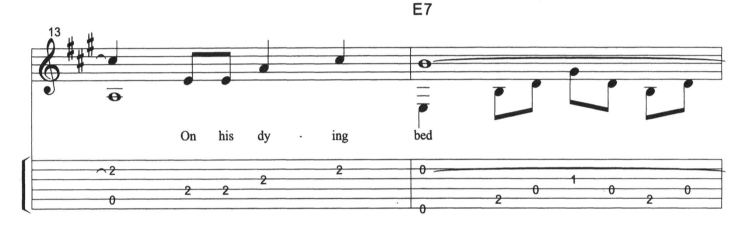

On his dy · ing bed

E7   A

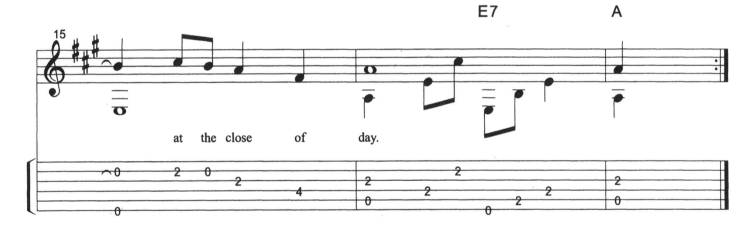

at the close of day.

2. "Oh bury me not on the lone prairie"
   Where the wild coyotes will howl o'er me,
   In a narrow grave just six by three.
   "Oh bury me not on the lone prairie."

3. "It matters not, I've oft been told,
   Where the body lies when the heart grows cold.
   Yet grant, oh, grant this wish to me:
   Oh, bury me not on the lone prairie."

4. "I've always wished to be laid when I died
   In the little churchyard on the green hillside;
   By my fathers grave there let mine be,
   And bury me not on the lone prairie."

5. "Let my death-slumber be where my mothers prayer
   And a sisters's tear will mingle there;
   Where my friends can come and weep o'er me.
   Oh, bury me not on the lone prairie."

6. "Oh, bury me not"--and his voice failed there,
   But we took no heed of his dying prayer.
   In a narrow grave just six by three,
   We buried him on the lone prairie.

7. And the cowboys now, as they roam the plain,
   For they marked the spot where his bones were lain,
   Fling a handful of roses o'er the grave,
   With a prayer to Him who his soul will save.

8. "Oh, bury me not on the lone prairie,
   Where the wolves can howl and growl o'er me.
   Fling a handful of roses o'er my grave,
   With a prayer to Him who my soul will save."

THE BRAZOS

TRADITIONAL

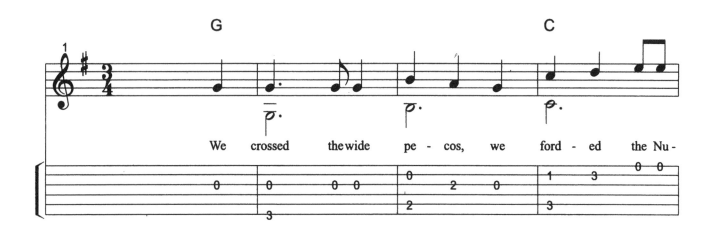

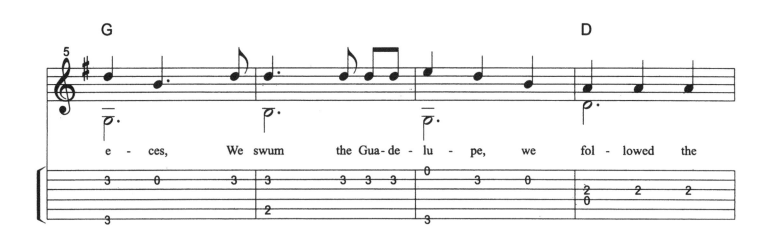

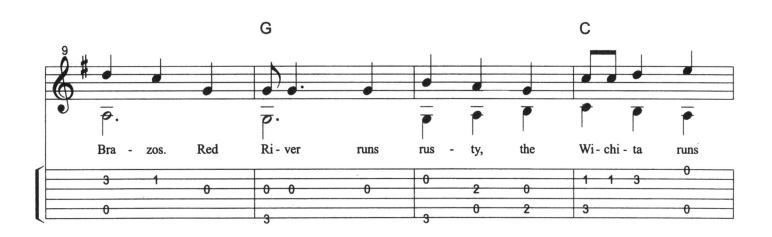

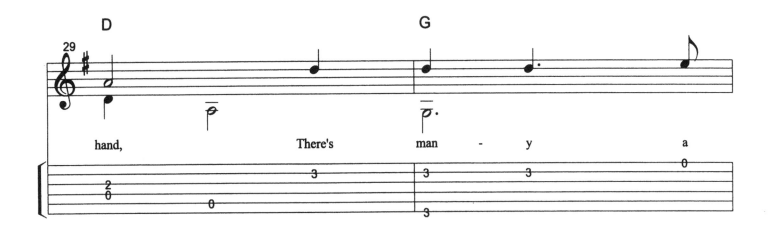

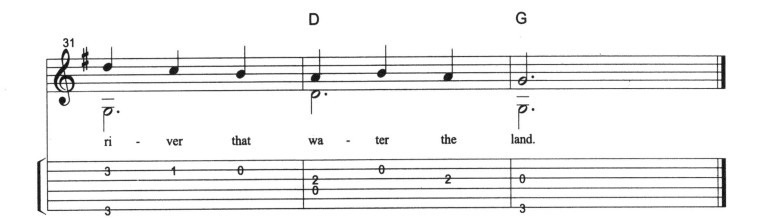

BUFFALO GALS

WORDS AND MUSIC BY COOL WHITE (JOHN HODGES)

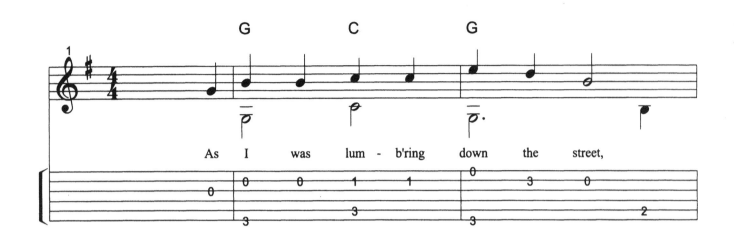

As I was lum - b'ring down the street,

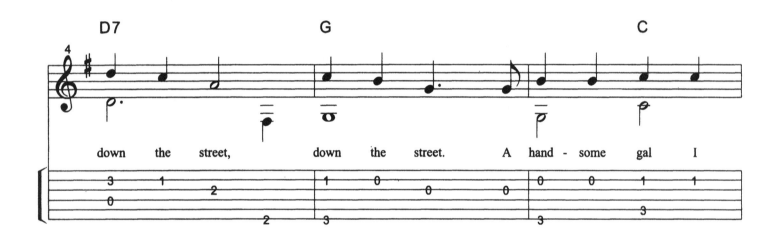

down the street, down the street. A hand - some gal I

chanced to meet, oh, she was fair to view.

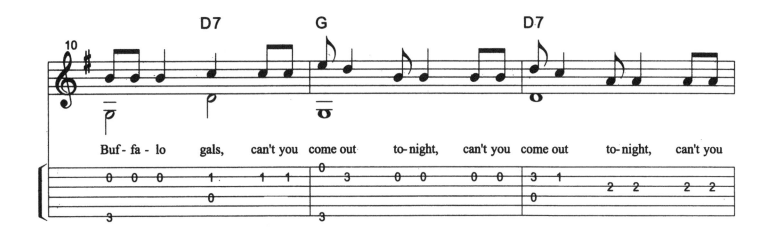

Buf - fa - lo gals, can't you come out to-night, can't you come out to-night, can't you

come out to-night? Buf - fa - lo gals, can't you come out to-night, and

dance by the light of the moon.

BLOOD ON THE SADDLE

TRADITIONAL

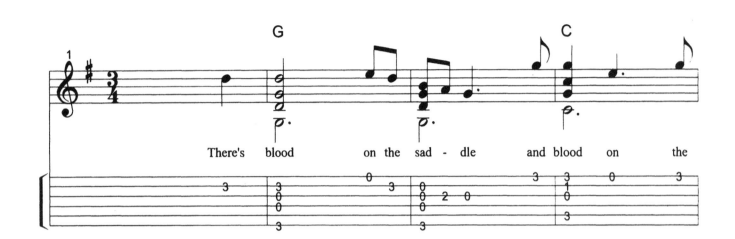

There's blood on the sad - dle and blood on the

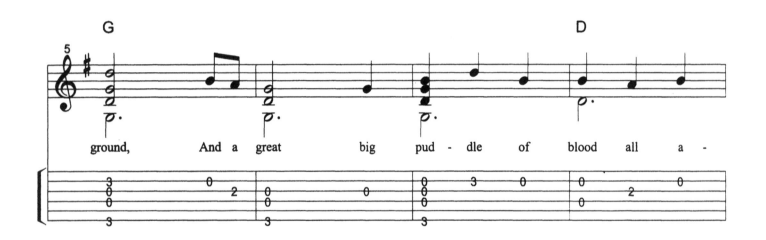

ground, And a great big pud - dle of blood all a -

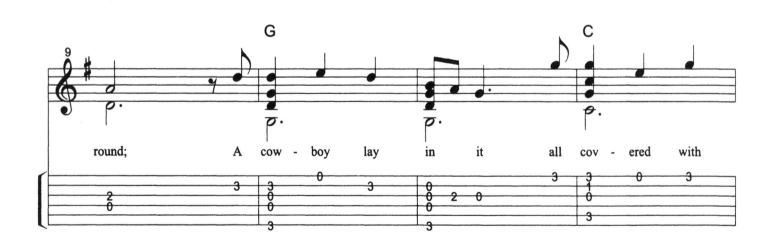

round; A cow - boy lay in it all cov - ered with

gore,　　And he nev - er will

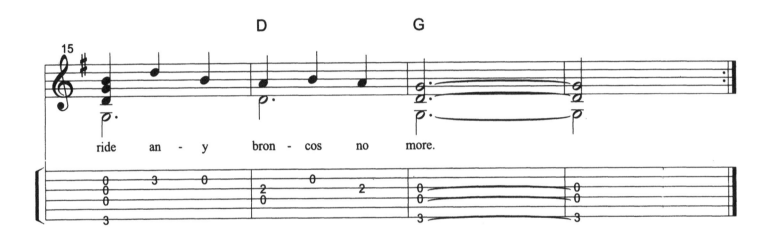

ride an - y bron - cos no more.

Oh, pity the cowboy all gory and red,
A bronco fell on him and bashed in his head.
There was blood on the saddle and blood on the ground,
And a great big puddle of blood all around.

CARELESS LOVE

TRADITIONAL

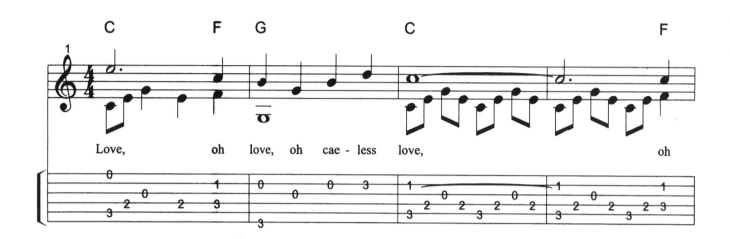

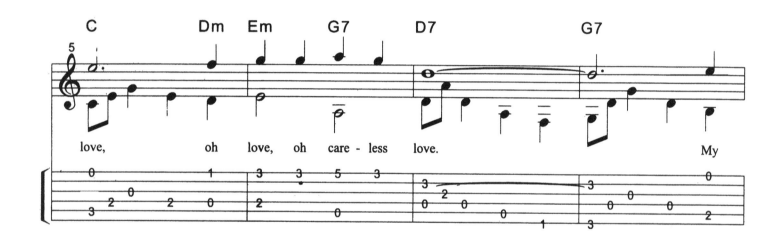

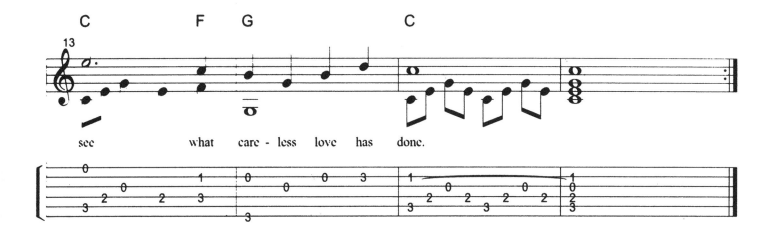

see   what   care - less   love   has   done.

I was happy as can be,
My days were sunny, bright and free.
You came along to do me wrong,
and you brought your careless love to me.

CATTLE CALL

TRADITIONAL

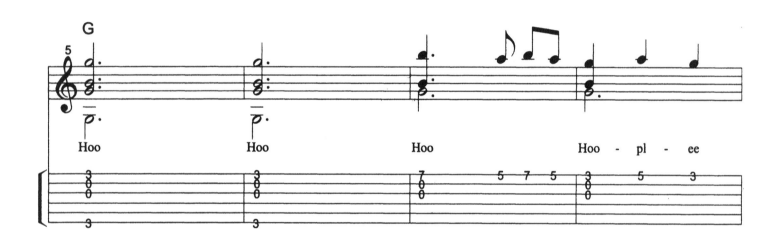

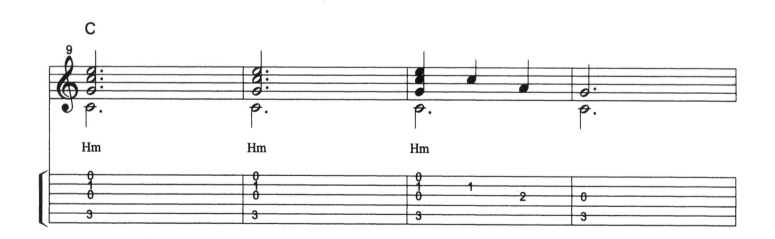

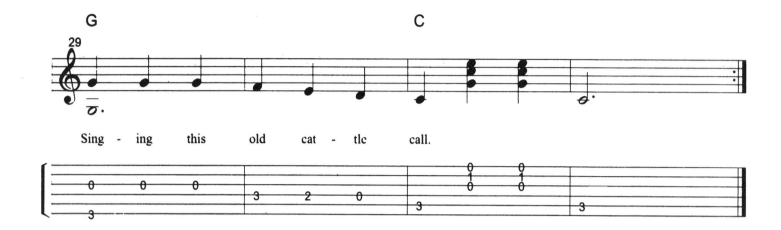

Sing - ing this old cat - tle call.

With my saddle all shedded and the cattle all bedded
Nothing wild seems to be wrong;
Make my bed 'neath the skies; I look up to the stars,
And then I can sing you this call

Well, each day I do ride o'er a range far and wide.
I'm goin' home this fall;
Well, I don't mind the weather, my hearts like a feather,
"Cause always I'll sing you this call

THE COLORADO TRAIL

TRADITIONAL

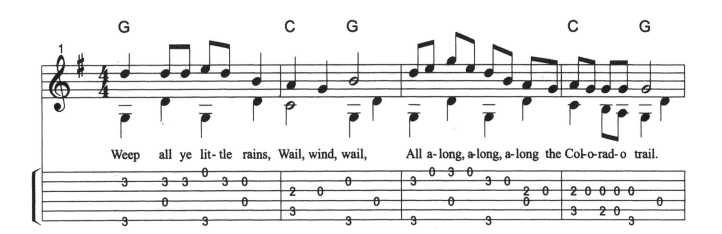

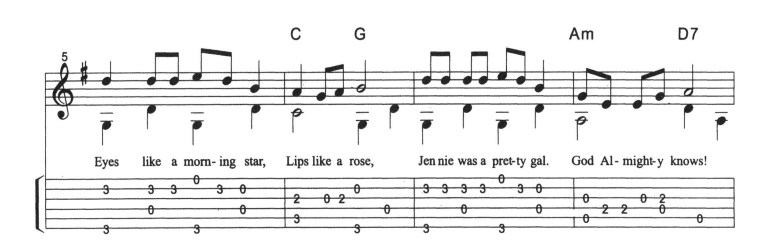

Weep all ye lit- tle rains, Wail, wind, wail, All a-long, a-long, a-long the Col-o-rad-o trail.

Eyes like a morn- ing star, Lips like a rose, Jen nie was a pret-ty gal. God Al-might-y knows!

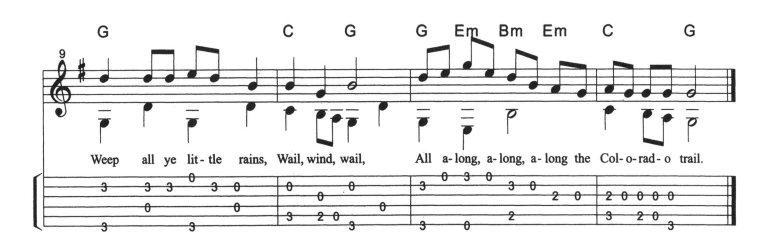

Weep all ye lit- tle rains, Wail, wind, wail, All a- long, a-long, a- long the Col-o-rad- o trail.

CLEMENTINE

WORDS AND MUSIC BY PERCY MONTROSE

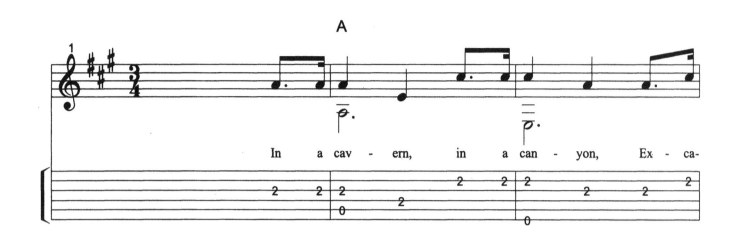

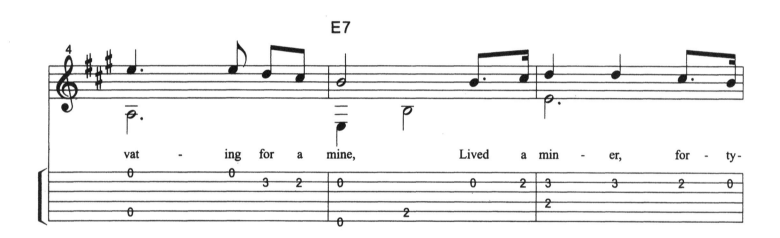

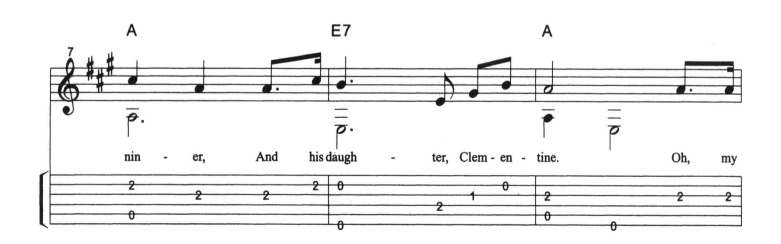

2. Light she was and, like a fairy.
   And her shoes were number nine ,
   Herring boxes, without topses,
   Sandals were for Clementine.

3. Drove she ducklings to the water,
   Ev'ry morning just at nine,
   Stubbed her toe upon a splinter,
   Fell into the foaming brine.

4. Ruby lips above the water,
   Blowing bubbles soft and fine,
   But alas, I was no swimmer,
   So I lost my Clementine.

5. There's a churchyard on the hillside,
   Where the flowers grow and twine,
   There grow roses 'mongst the posies,
   Fertilized by Clementine

6. Then the miner, forty-niner,
   Soon began to peak and pine;
   Thought he ought to join his daughter,
   Now he's with his Clementine.

7. In my dreams she still doth haunt me,
   Robed in garments soaked in brine;
   Though in life I used to hug her,
   Now she's dead I draw the line.

THE COWBOY'S DREAM

TRADITIONAL

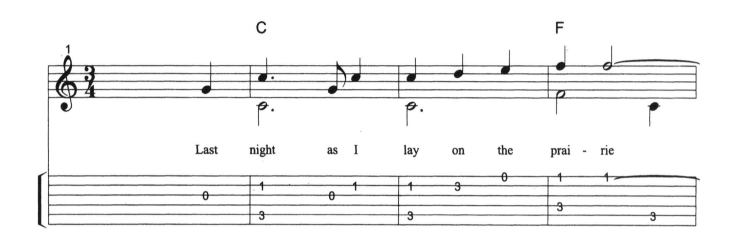

Last night as I lay on the prai - rie

And looked at the stars in the sky,

I won - dered if ev - er a cow - boy,

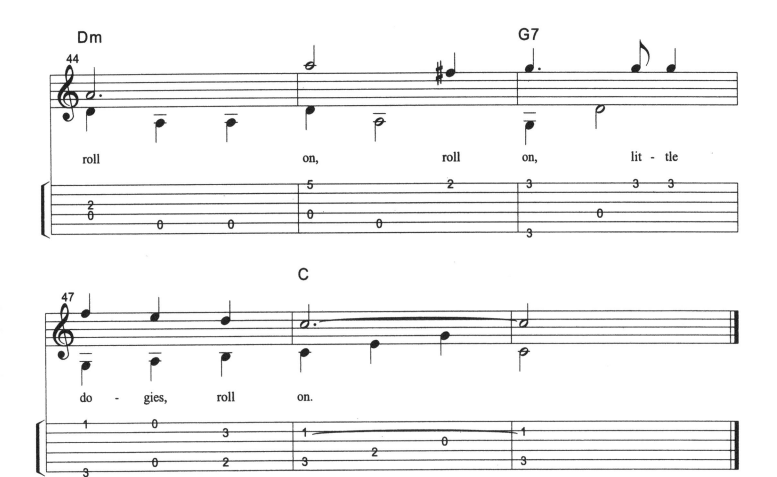

roll on, roll on, lit - tle
do - gies, roll on.

2. And I'm scared that I'll be a stray yearling,
   A maverick unbranded on high;
   And get out in the bunch with the "rustles"
   When the Boss of the Riders goes by.

   Chorus

3. For they tell of another big owner,
   Who's ne'er overstocked, so they say,
   But who always makes room for the sinner
   Who drifts from the straight, narrow way.

   Chorus

4. They say that he will never forget you,
   That he knows every action and look;
   So, for safety, you'd better get branded,
   Have your name in the great Tally Book.

   Chorus

THE COWBOY'S SOLILOQUY

WORDS AND MUSIC BY CARL T. SPRAGUE

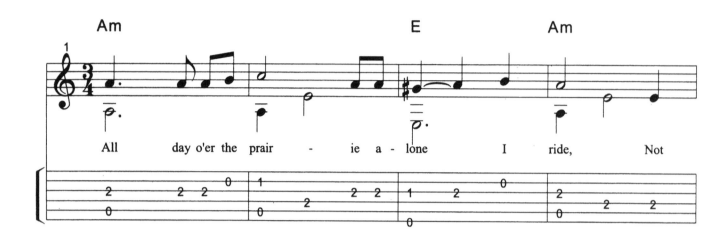

All day o'er the prair - ie a - lone I ride, Not

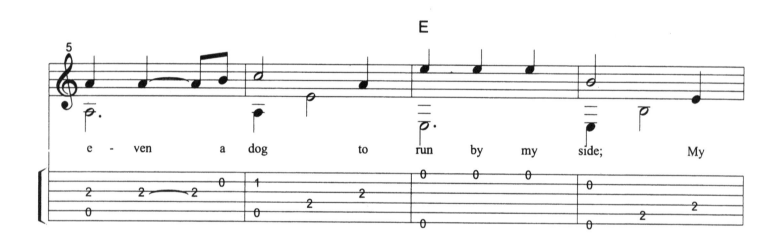

e - ven a dog to run by my side; My

fi - re I kin - dle with chips ga - thered round, And

wipe   on   a   sack,   And   car - ry   my

ward - robe   all   on   my   back.

2. My ceiling the sky, my carpet the grass,
   My music the lowing of herds as they pass;
   My books are the brooks, my sermons the stones,
   My parson's a wolf on a pulpit of bones.
   But then if my cooking ain't very complete,
   Hygienists can't blame me for living to eat;
   And where is the man who sleeps more profound
   Than the cowboy who stretches himself on the ground.

3. My books teach me constancy ever to prize,
   My sermons that small things I should not despise;
   And my parson's remarks from his pulpit of bone,
   Is that "the Lord favours those who look out for their own."
   Between love and me lies a gulf very wide,
   And a luckier fellow may call her his bride;
   But cupid is always a friend to the bold,
   And the best of his arrows are pointed with gold.

THE GIRL I LEFT BEHIND ME

WORDS AND MUSIC BY THOMAS MOORE

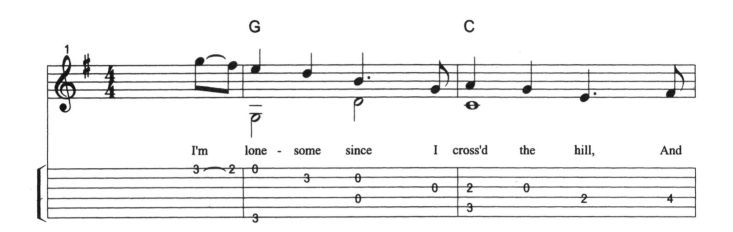

I'm lone - some since I cross'd the hill, And

o'er the moor and val - ley; Such heav - y thoughts my

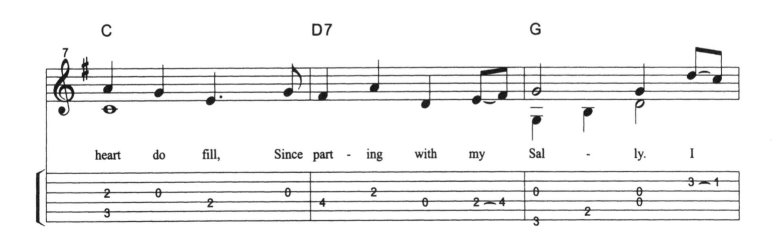

heart do fill, Since part - ing with my Sal - ly. I

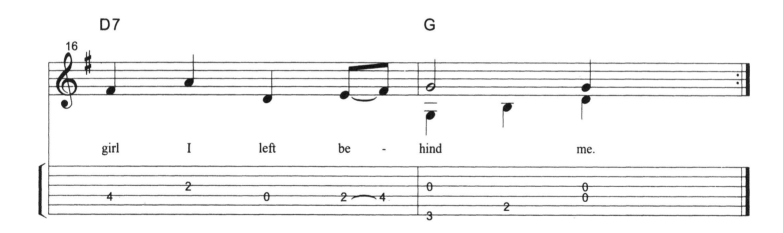

2. Oh, ne'er shall I forget the night, The stars were bright above me,
   And gently lent their silv'ry light, When first she vowed she loved me,
   But now I'm bound to army camp, Kind Heav'n, may favor find me,
   And send me safely back again To the girl I left behind me.

3. The bee shall honey taste no more, The dove become a ranger,
   The dashing waves shall cease to roar Ere she's to me a stranger;
   The vows we've register'd above Shall ever cheer and bind me,
   In constancy to her I love, The girl I left behind me.

4. My mind her form shall still retain In sleeping or in waking,
   Until I see my love again, For whom my heart is breaking.
   If ever I should see the day When Mars shall have resigned me,
   For evermore I'll gladly stay With the girl I left behind me.

DOWN IN THE VALLEY

TRADITIONAL

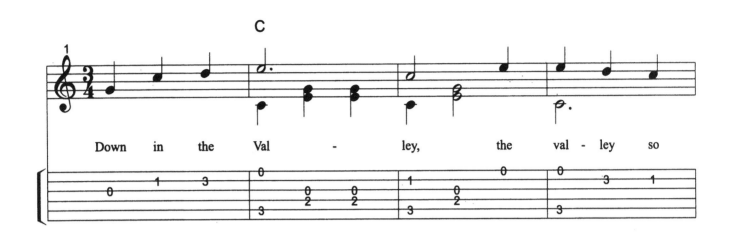

Down in the Val - ley, the val - ley so

low, Hang your head o

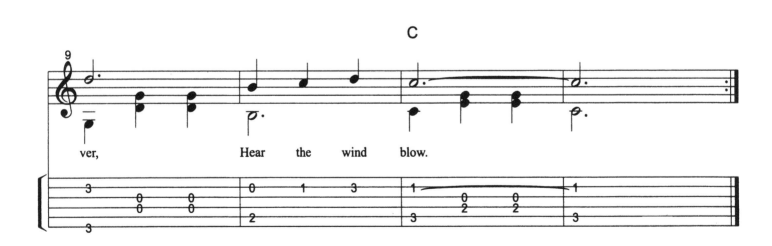

ver, Hear the wind blow.

Hear the wind blow, love, Oh hear the wind blow,
Hang your head over, hear the wind blow.

Give my heart ease, love oh give my heart ease,
Think of me, darling, oh give my heart ease.

Write me a letter and send it to me,
Care of the jailhouse in Raleigh, N.C.

Write me a letter with just a few lines,
An-swer me, darling, and say you'll be mine.

Roses love sunshine and violets love dew,
Angels in Heaven know I love you!

This gloomy prison is far from you, dear,
But not forever, I'm out in a year.

I make this promise to go straight and true,
And for a lifetime to love only you.

THE EYES OF TEXAS ARE UPON YOU

WORDS AND MUSIC BY JOHN L. SINCLAIR

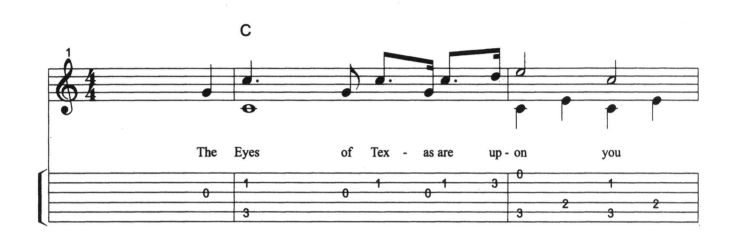

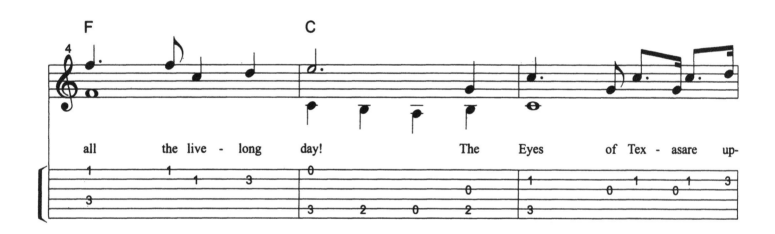

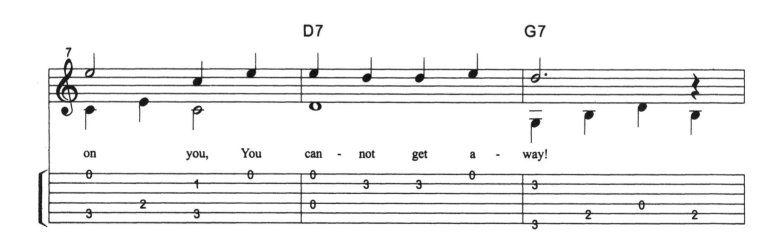

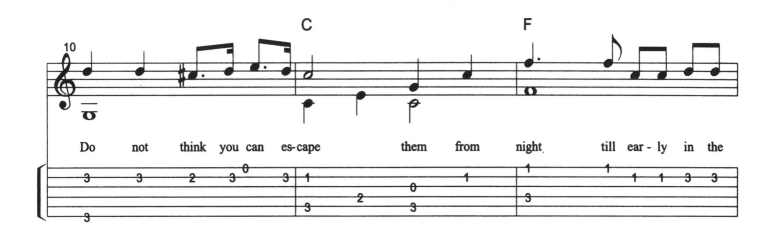

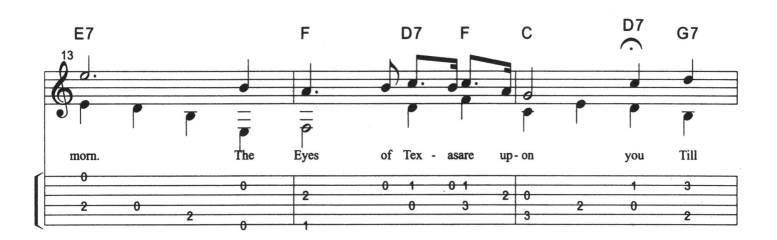

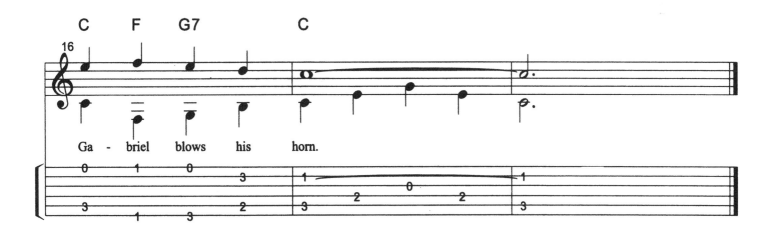

FRANKIE AND JOHNNY

TRADITIONAL

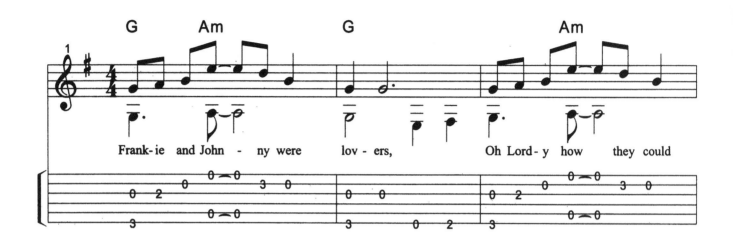

Frank-ie and John - ny were lov - ers, Oh Lord- y how they could

love. They swore to be true to each oth - er,

True as the stars a - bove, He was her man,

2. Frankie, she was a good woman, As everybody knows,
   Spent a hundred dollars, Just to buy her man some clothes,
   He was her man, but he done her wrong.

3. Frankie went down to the corner, Just for a bucket of beer,
   Said to the fat bartender, "Has my loving Johnny been here?
   He was my man, but he's doin' me wrong."

4. "Now I don't want to tell you no stories, And I don't want to tell you no lies.
   I saw your man about an hour ago with a gal named Nellie Bly.
   He was your man, but he's doin' you wrong,"

5. Frankie,she went down to the hotel, Didn't go there for fun.
   Under her long, red kimono she carried a forty-four gun.
   He was her man, but he done her wrong.

6. Frankie looked over the transom to see what she could spy.
   There sat Johnny on the sofa, Just loving up Nellie Bly.
   He was her man, but he done her wrong.

7. Frankie got down from that high stool, She didn't want to see no more.
   Rooty-toot-toot, three times she shot right through that hardwood door.
   He was her man, but he done her wrong.

8. Sixteen rubber-tired hearses, Sixteen rubber-tired hacks,
   They take poor Johnny to the graveyard, They ain't gonna bring him back.
   He was her man, but he done her wrong.

9. The judge said to the jury, "It's as plain as plain can be,
   This woman shot her lover, It's murder in the first degree."
   He was her man, but he done her wrong.

10. Frankie mounted the scaffold, As calm as a girl can be,
    And turning her eyes to heaven, She said, "Good Lord, I'm comin' to Thee."
    He was her man, but he done her wrong.

11. This story has no moral, This story has no end,
    This story only goes to show that there ain't no good in men!
    He was her man, but he done her wrong.

GIT ALONG, LITTLE DOGIES (Whoopee Ti Yi Yo)

TRADITIONAL

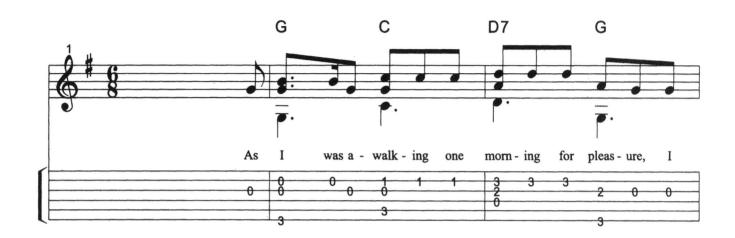

As I was a-walk-ing one morn-ing for pleas-ure, I

spied a cow-punch-er a rid-ing a-long. His hat was throwed back and his

Chorus

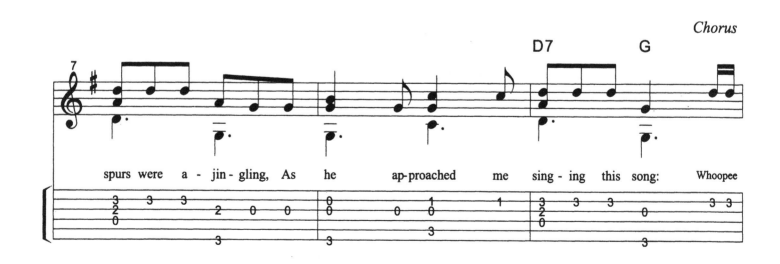

spurs were a-jin-gling, As he ap-proached me sing-ing this song: Whoopee

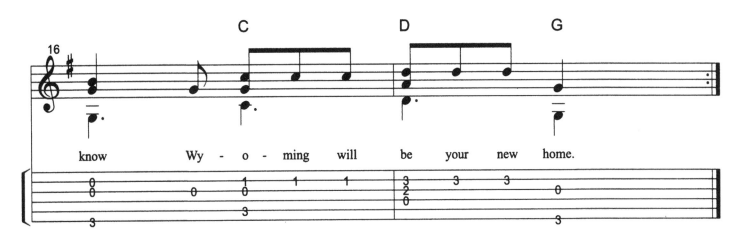

2. It's early in spring that we round up the dogies, And mark 'em and brand 'em and cut off thier tales.
   We round up our horses and load on the chuck wagon, And throw the dogies out onto the trail.
   Chorus

3. It's whoopin' and yellin' and drivin' them dogies, Oh, how I wish that you would go on.
   It's whoopin' and punchin' and go on, little dogies, For you know Wyoming will be your new home.
   Chorus

4. Your mother she was raised a-way down in Texas, Where the jimson weed and sandburs grow.
   Now we'll fill you up on prickley pear and cholla, Till you are ready for the trail to Idaho.
   Chorus

5. Oh, you'll be soup for Uncle Sam's Injuns, "It's beef, heap beef," I hear them cry.
   Git along, git along, git along, little dogies, You're going to be beef steers by and by.
   Chorus

GOODBYE, OLD PAINT

TRADITIONAL

Chorus

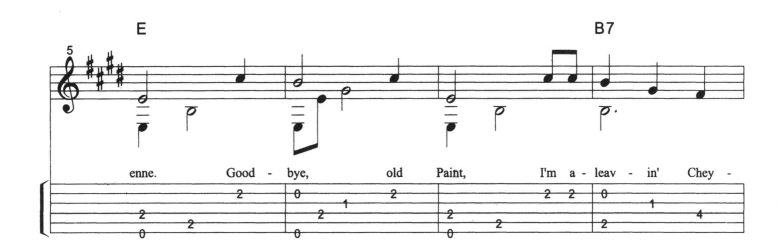

Verse

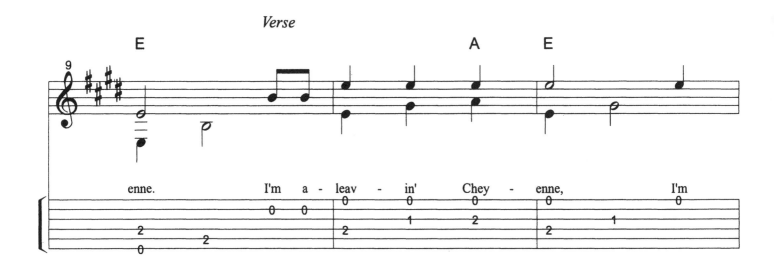

43

2. My foot in the stirrup, my pony won't stand, Goodbye old paint, I'm leavin' Cheyenne.
Chorus

3. Old Paints a good pony, he paces when he can, Goodbye, little Annie, I'm off to Montan'.
Chorus

4. Oh, hitch up your horses and feed 'em some hay, And seat yourself by me so long as you stay.
Chorus

5. My horses ain't hungry, they'll not eat your hay, My wagon is loaded and rolling away.
Chorus

6. Oh, when I die, take my saddle from the wall, Put it on my pony, lead him from the stall.
Chorus

7. Tie my bones to his back, turn our faces to the west, And we'll ride the prairie that we love the best.
Chorus

HOME ON THE RANGE

WORDS BY BREWSTER HIGLEY
MUSIC BY DAN KELLY

Oh, give me a home where the buf - fa - lo

roam, Where the deer and the an - te - lope play,

Where sel - dom is heard a dis - cour - ag - ing

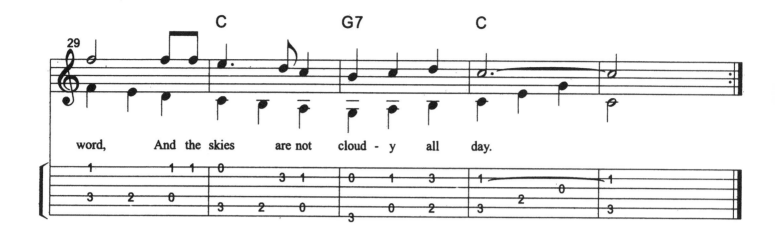

word,　And the skies　are not　cloud - y　all　day.

2. How often at night, when the heavens are bright,
   With the light of the glittering stars,
   Have I stood there amazed, and asked as I gazed
   If their glory exceeds that of ours.
   Chorus

3. Oh, give me a land where the bright diamond sand
   Flows leisurely down the stream,
   Where a graceful white swan goes gliding along,
   Like a maid in a heavenly dream.
   Chorus

4. Oh, I love those wild flowers in this dear land of ours,
   The curlew, I love to hear scream,
   And I love the white rocks and the antelope flocks
   That gaze on the mountain so green.
   Chorus

5. Where the air is so pure and the zephyres so free,
   The breezes so balmy and light,
   That I would not exchange my home on the range
   For all of the cities so bright.
   Chorus

LITTLE JOE, THE WRANGLER

WORDS AND MUSIC BY JACK THORP

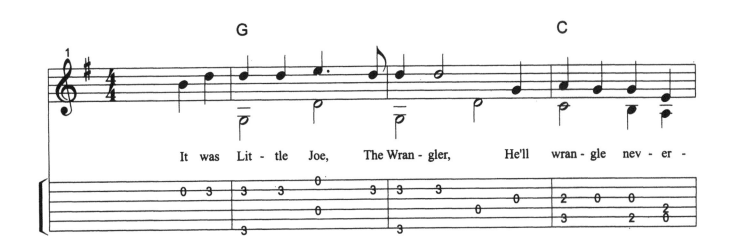

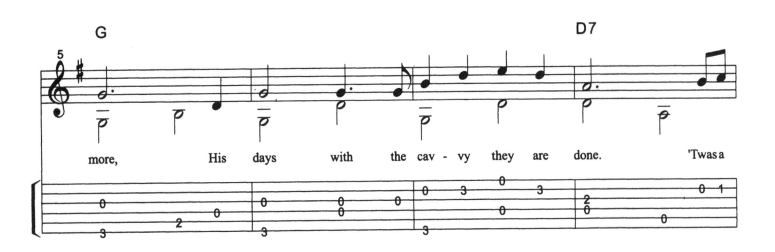

life had seen be - fore.

2. His saddle was a Southern kack built many years ago
   And an O.K. spur from one foot idly hung,
   While the hot roll in the cotton sack was loosely tied behind
   And a canteen from the saddle horn was slung.
   He left his home in Texas, his ma had married twice,
   And his old man beat him every day or two,
   So he saddled up old chaw one night and lit a chuck this way,
   Thought he'd try and paddle noe his own canoe.

IDA RED

TRADITIONAL

Light the pi-lot fire in the grate Clock on the man-tle

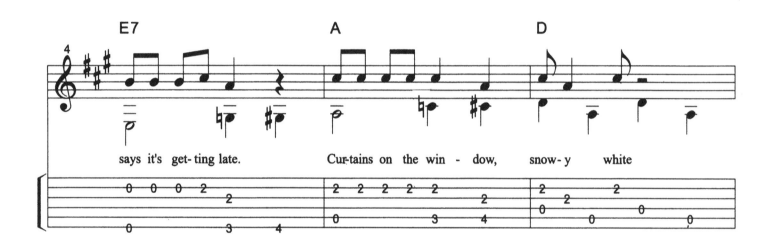

says it's get-ting late. Cur-tains on the win - dow, snow-y white

Chorus

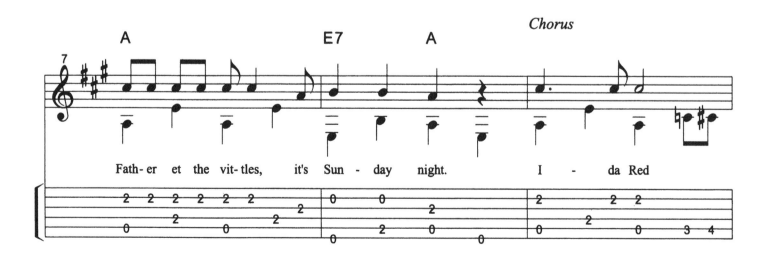

Fath-er et the vit-tles, it's Sun - day night. I - da Red

2. Lamp on the table, picture on the wall,
   There's a pretty soul and thats not all.
   If i'm not mistaken and I'm sure I'm right,
   there's somebody else in the parlour tonight.
   Chorus

3. Chicken in a bread bin pickin' out dough
   Granny whatta ya know about Ohio?
   Hurry up boys and don't fool around
   Grab your partner and truck on down.
   Chorus

4. My old Missus swore to me
   when she died she'd set me free
   she lived so long her head got bald
   She took a notion not to die at all.
   Chorus

5. Repeat verse 2 then Chorus

JOHN HARDY

TRADITIONAL

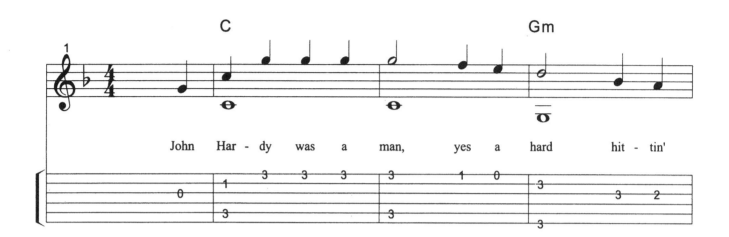

John Har-dy was a man, yes a hard hit-tin'

man, His pis-tol was his pal night and day.

He shot and he killed and as quick-ly up and

ran, While the crowd saw John Har - dy get-tin' a - way, Oh

Lord, All the crowd saw John Har - dy gettin' a - way.

2. John Hardy was a man, you could never decieve,
   He held a pair of aces one day.
   Bill Jones had three kings, one was hidden in his sleeve,
   And they buried poor Bill the following day, Oh Lord,
   And they all saw John Harding gettin' away.

3. John Hardy might have lived as a free man today,
   Except for one mistake he made,
   He went to see if his family was O.K.,
   And the law was a-waitin' out in the shade, Oh Lord!
   And the law was a law that had to be paid.

4. John Hardy called himself a fair-fightin' man,
   He said he had good reason to kill.
   He once ripped an arm from saloonkeeper, Dan,
   'Cause he sold watered whiskey out of a still, Oh Lord!
   Hardy bought watered whiskey out of a still.

5. John Hardy spoke these words with a noose 'round his neck,
   "My absence won't make anyone grieve.
   If this be the price, guess I'll have to pay the check,
   But I lost 'cause a card was up in his sleeve, Oh Lord!
   And John Hardy, he 'lows no card in a sleeve."

LILY OF THE WEST

TRADITIONAL

When first I came to Louis - ville, Some pleas - ure there to

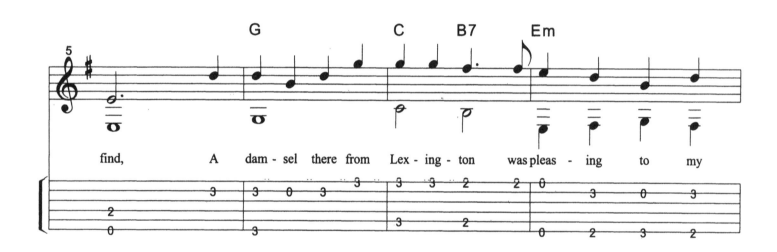

find, A dam - sel there from Lex - ing - ton was pleas - ing to my

mind. Her ros - y cheeks, her ru - by lips like ar - rows pierced my

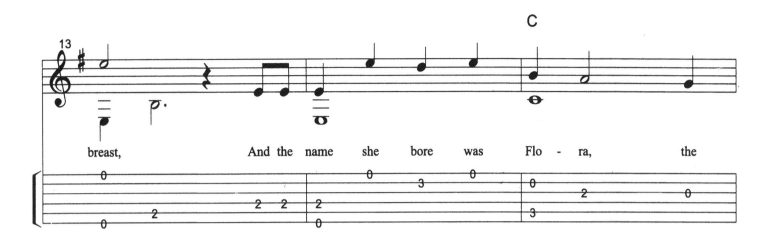

breast,   And the name   she   bore   was   Flo - ra,   the

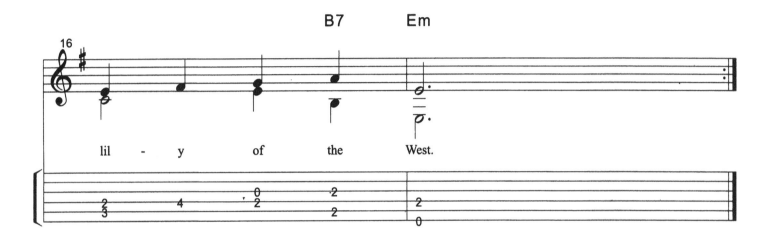

lil - y   of   the   West.

2. I courted lovely Flora, and to her I was so kind,
But she went to another man, It nearly wrecked my mind.
She robbed me of my freedom and deprived me of my rest,
Betrayed was I by Flora, the lily of the West.

3. He met her in a shady grove, this man of high degree,
I saw him kiss my Flora and it sure did things to me.
She told me he was just a friend, but still I was depressed,
Betrayed was I by Flora, the lily of the West.

4. I stepped up to my rival with my dagger in my hand,
I siezed him by the collar, it's not hard to understand,
That, blinded by my jealousy, I pierce him in the breast,
Betrayed was I by Flora, the lily of the West.

5. The trial was held, I made a plea, but 'twas of no avail,
Now I await the hangman in a stinkin' rotten jail.
But, though I give my all away and though my life is messed,
I love my faithless Flora, the lily of the West.

LONE STAR TRAIL

TRADITIONAL

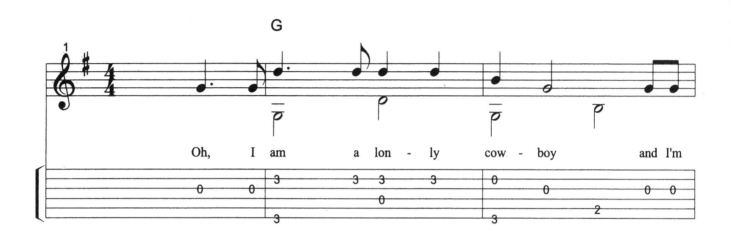

NIGHTTIME IN NEVADA

TRADITIONAL

When it's night - time in Ne - va - da I'm dreamin'

Of the old days on the de - sert and you.

I miss you when the camp - fires are gleam - in',

62

I hope that we will meet a - gain some day.

THE OLD CHISHOLM TRAIL

TRADITIONAL

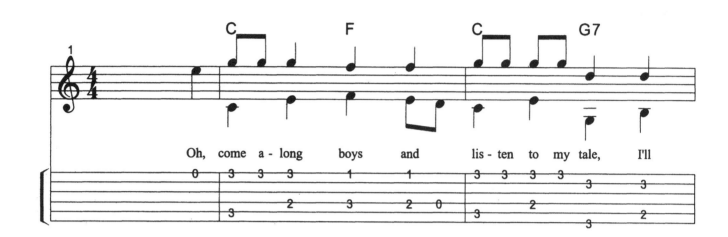

Oh, come a - long boys and lis - ten to my tale, I'll

Chorus

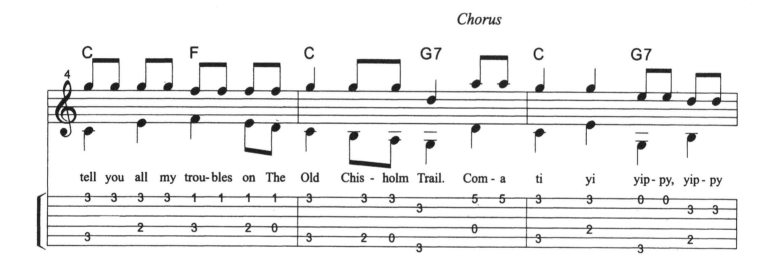

tell you all my trou - bles on The Old Chis - holm Trail. Com - a ti yi yip - py, yip - py

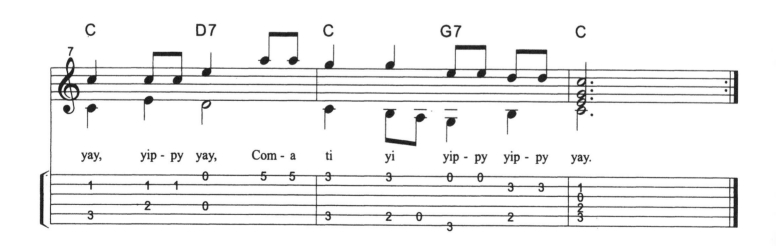

yay, yip - py yay, Com - a ti yi yip - py yip - py yay.

2. I started up the trail on October twenty third,
   I started up the trail with the Lone Star herd.
   Chorus:

3 I woke up in the morning on the old Chisholm trail
   With a rope in one hand and a cow by the tail.
   Chorus:

4. I'm up in the morning before daylight
   And before I sleep the moon shines bright.
   Chorus:

5. It's bacon and beans most ev'ry day,
   I'd just as soon be eatin' prairie hay.
   Chorus:

6. It's cloudy in the west and a-lookin' like rain
   And my durned old slickers in the wagon again.
   Chorus:

7. I'm going back to town to draw my money,
   I'm going back home to see my honey.
   Chorus:

8. I went to the boss to draw my roll,
   He had me figured out nine dollars in the hole.
   Chorus:

9. I'll sell my outfit just as soon as I can,
   and I won't punch cattle for any man.
   Chorus

10. With my knees in the saddle and my home in the sky,
    I'll quite punching cows in the sweet bye and bye.
    Chorus:

THE OLD OAKEN BUCKET

WORDS BY SAMUEL WOODWORTH
MUSIC BY GEORGE KIALLMARK

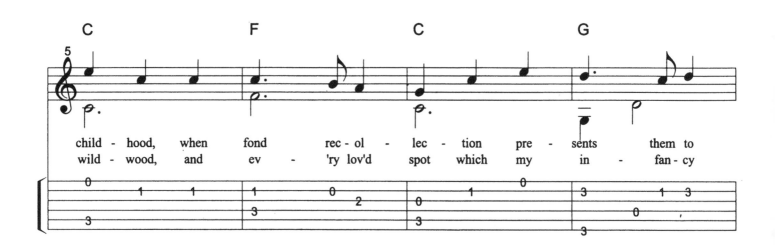

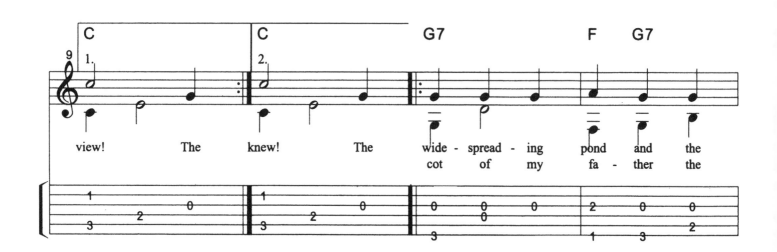

ON TOP OF OLD SMOKEY

TRADITIONAL

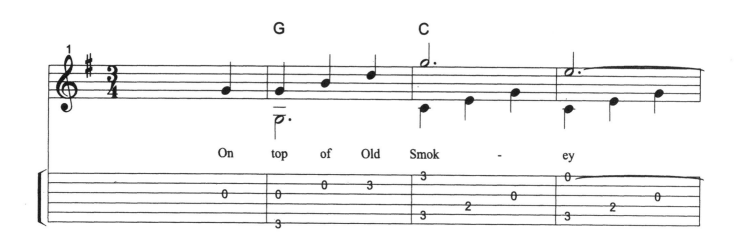

On   top   of   Old   Smok -   ey

all   cov - ered   with   snow,   I

lost   my   true   lov - er   for

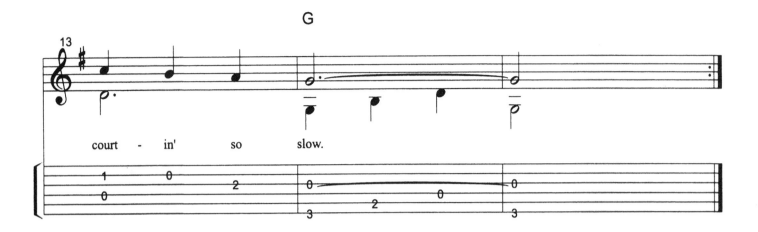

court - in' so slow.

2. For courtings a pleasure and parting is grief,
   And a false hearted lover is worse than a thief.

3. A thief will just rob you and take what you have,
   But a false hearted lover will lead you to the grave.

4. And the grave will decay you and turn you to dust,
   Not one boy in a hundred a poor girl can trust.

RED RIVER VALLEY

TRADITIONAL

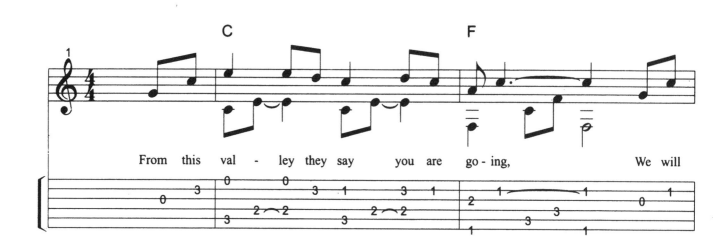

From this val - ley they say you are go - ing, We will

miss your bright eyes and sweet smile, For they say you are tak - ing the

sun - shine, That has bright - en'd our path - ways a - while.

Chorus:
> Come and sit by my side if you love me,
> Do not hasten to bid adieu.
> Just remember the Red River Valley,
> And the cowboy who loved you so true.

2. Won't you think of the valley you're leaving?
   Oh, how lonely and sad it will be.
   Do you think of the kind hearts you're breaking,
   And the pain you are causing to me?

3. As you go to your home by the ocean,
   May you never forget those sweet hours,
   That we spent in the Red River Valley,
   And the love we exchanged 'mid the flowers.

SWEET BETSY FROM PIKE

WORDS AND MUSIC BY JOHN A. STONE

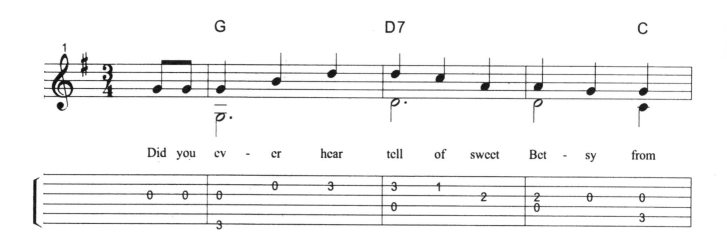

Did you ev - er hear tell of sweet Bet - sy from

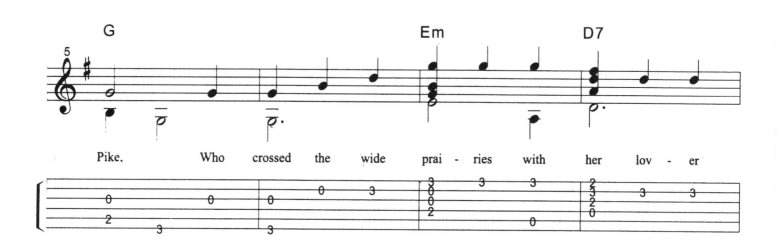

Pike, Who crossed the wide prai - ries with her lov - er

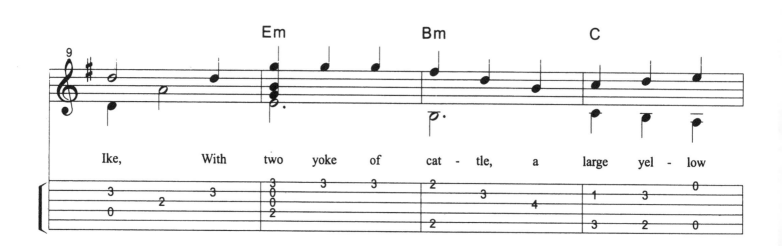

Ike, With two yoke of cat - tle, a large yel - low

2. One evening quite early they camped on the Platte,
   'Twas near by the road on a green shady flat,
   Where Betsy, quite tired, lay down to repose,
   With wonder Ike gazed at the Pike County rose.
   Chorus

3. They soon reached the desert, where Betsy gave out,
   And down in the sand she lay rolling about,
   While Ike, half distracted, looked on in surprise,
   Saying, "Betsy get up, you'll get sand in your eyes."
   Chorus

4. Sweet Betsy got up in a great deal of pain,
   Declared she'd go back to Pike County again.
   But Ike gave a sigh, and they fondly embraced,
   And they traveled along with his arm 'round her waist.
   Chorus

5. The Shanghai ran off and thier cattle all died,
   That morning the last piece of bacon was fried,
   Poor Ike was discouraged and Betsy got mad,
   The dog dropped his tail and looked wondrously sad.
   Chorus

6. They swam the wide rivers and crossed the tall peaks,
   They camped on the prairy for weeks upon weeks,
   Starvation and cholera, hard work and slaughter,
   To reach California spite hell or high water.
   Chorus

7. One morning they stopped on a very high hill,
   With wonder looked down upon old Placerville.
   Ike shouted and said as he cast his eye's down,
   "Sweet Betsy, my darling, we've got to Hangtown."
   Chorus

TOM DOOLEY

TRADITIONAL

Hang down your head, Tom Doo - ley, Hang down your head and

cry, You killed poor Lau - ra Fos - ter,

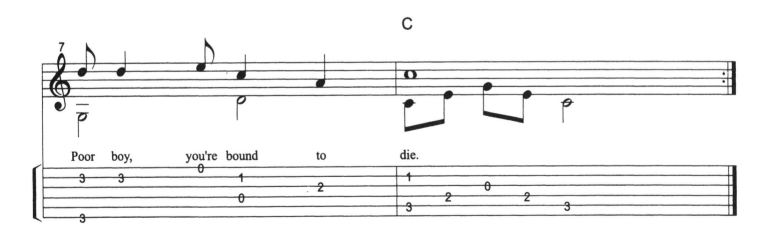

Poor boy, you're bound to die.

1. I met her on the mountain, I swore she'd be my wife,
   I met her on the mountain, And I stabbed her with my knife.
   Chorus

2. When this time comes tomorrow, I reckon that I'll be,
   In some lonesome valley, A-hangin' from a white oak tree.
   Chorus

THE STREETS OF LAREDO (THE COWBOY'S LAMENT)

WORDS BY JACK THORP
MUSIC BY MYRA E. HULL

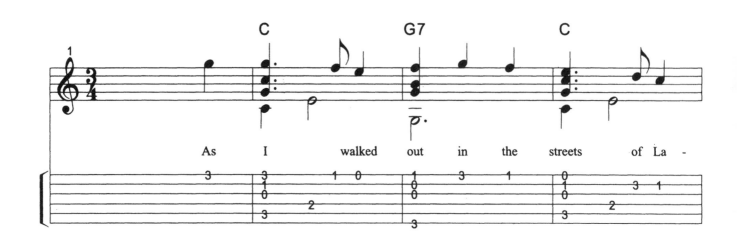

As I walked out in the streets of La-

re - do, As I waalked out in La - re - do one

day, I spied a poor cow - boy all wrapped in white

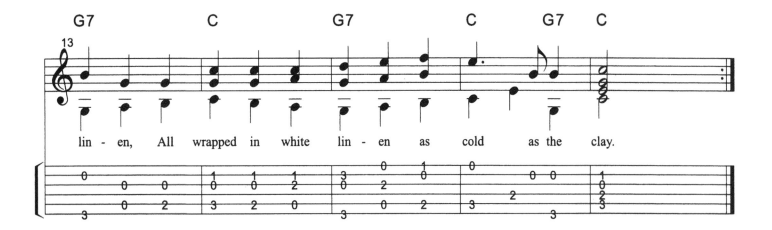

2. "I see by your outfir that you are a cowboy",
   These words he did say as I calmly walked by.
   "Come sit down beside me and hear my sad story,
   I'm shot in the breast and I know I must die."

3. "It was once in the saddle I used to go dashing,
   With no one as quick on the trigger as I.
   I sat in a card game in back of the barroom,
   Got shot in the back and today I must die."

4. "Get six of my buddies to carry my coffin,
   And six pretty maidens to sing a sad song,
   Take me to the valley and lay the sod o'er me,
   For I'm a young cowboy who played the game wrong."

5. "Oh, beat the drum slowly and play the fife lowly,
   And play the dead march as they carry my pall.
   Put bunches of roses all over my coffin,
   The roses will deaden the clods as they fall."

6. "Go gather around you a crowd of young cowboys,
   And tell them the story of this my sad fate.
   Tell one and the other before they go further,
   To stop thier wild roving before it's to late."

7. "Go fetch me a cup, just a cup of cold water,
   To cool my parched lips," the cowboy then said.
   Before I returned, his brave spirit left him,
   And, gone to his maker, the cowboy was dead.

THE YELLOW ROSE OF TEXAS

TRADITIONAL

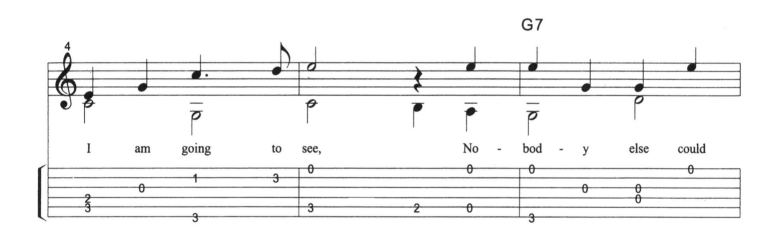

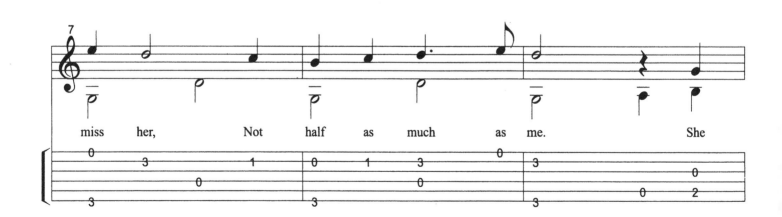